OXFAM

Sean Connolly

FRANKLIN WATTS
LONDON•SYDNEY

 An Appleseed Editions book

Paperback edition 2010

First published in 2008 by Franklin Watts
338 Euston Road, London NW1 3BH

Franklin Watts Australia
Hachette Children's Books
Level 17/207 Kent St, Sydney, NSW 2000

Created by Appleseed Editions Ltd,
Well House, Friars Hill, Guestling,
East Sussex TN35 4ET

Designed by Helen James
Edited by Mary-Jane Wilkins
Picture research by Su Alexander

ISBN 978 1 4451 0100 2

Dewey Classification: 361.763

A CIP catalogue for this book is available from the British Library.

Photograph acknowledgements
page 6 Mike F. Alquinto/EPA/Corbis; 8 The Oxfam Archive; 11 Hulton-Deutsch
Collection/Corbis; 13 Rudy Sulgan/Corbis; 14 The Oxfam Archive; 16 James
Robert Fuller/Corbis; 18 Howard Davies/Oxfam; 21 & 23 Jerry Carreon/Oxfam;
24 Charles E. Rotkin/Corbis; 26 Luc Gnago/Reuters/Corbis; 27 John Van Hasselt/
Sygma/Corbis; 28 Bernd Settnik/DPA/Corbis; 30 Greg Williams/Oxfam;
33 Peter Macdiarmid/Getty Images; 37 Philip Richardson; Gallo Images/Corbis;
38 Collart Herve/Corbis Sygma; 40 Kim Rowe/Oxfam; 42 Toby Adamson/Oxfam;
43 STR/EPA/Corbis
Front cover Howard Davies/Oxfam

Printed in Hong Kong

Franklin Watts is a division of Hachette Children's Books,
an Hachette UK company.
www.hachette.co.uk

CONTENTS

Who suffers most in a disaster?

Think of the disasters we see in the news: earthquakes, famine, hurricanes, floods and tsunamis. Some of these tragedies affect people on a huge scale, killing hundreds or even thousands and leaving more people injured or without homes. And these are just the natural disasters, events once called 'acts of God'.

Even today, billions of people suffer from overcrowding, poverty and ill health.

As well as these natural events, the world faces many terrors caused by humans. Wars and conflicts, political oppression and organized hatred add to the human death toll every year. Many millions have lost their lives during the last hundred years – the same century in which so much progress was made in making people's lives safer and easier.

The victims

The people who suffer most from these natural or man-made crises are those who are poor. They are the people who become caught up in the crossfire during battles, or in volcano danger zones because they do not have the means to move to safer places. People who are not well off cannot afford to improve their homes, or protect them against earthquakes, floods or storms.

Many international organizations aim to help the victims of such troubles. One of these groups, Oxfam, concentrates on the link between poverty and suffering. If we recognize this link and undo it, the world will become a healthier, safer place.

International teamwork

Oxfam began in one of the world's richest countries – the United Kingdom – and it encouraged people in other well-off countries to form similar groups. But Oxfam is not about handouts passed on to the less fortunate every now and then when richer countries find the time. It is about teamwork and finding the link between all of the world's people.

Teamwork gives Oxfam a presence in more than 100 countries with the greatest need. By working with local people, Oxfam helps these countries to improve their own living conditions. And until the poor have a voice of their own, Oxfam makes their case in the international arena.

As Oxfam's website points out, 'there is no excuse for poverty in the 21st century. Our world has enough food and other resources for everyone.' But until these resources are shared out fairly, there is a need for organizations which push for such change. Oxfam is leading the way in making a difference.

Wartime roots

The name Oxfam often conjures up two different images – one familiar and local and the other linked to events in far-away countries. Most people have seen Oxfam shops in their local shopping precinct or high street, and they are as familiar as the local butcher or newsagent. Oxfam is also known to be a constant presence in disaster zones or during other emergencies everywhere in the world.

The first-ever Oxfam Shop opened at 17 Broad Street, Oxford, in 1948, when the charity was known as the Oxford Committee for Famine Relief.

Neither of these images tells the whole story, but together they form an image of a local organization with operations around the world. Oxfam has 700 shops staffed by 20,000 volunteers in the United Kingdom, which makes it part of the urban British landscape. But the familiar British Oxfam is just one of 13 members of the wider organization, Oxfam International. It is this international network which responds to disasters, helps poorer countries develop and builds links with governments and other organizations around the world.

Crisis in Greece

The story of Oxfam goes back to the Second World War. German forces defeated Greece early in the war, and in 1941 the Allies set up a naval blockade around Greece. The blockade was intended to stop military supplies from reaching the German forces in Greece. Unfortunately, the people of Greece – who have depended on sea trade for thousands of years – began to suffer badly.

Many concerned people in Britain worried about the Greek people, and the possibility that they faced famine without outside help. On 5 October 1942, the Oxford Committee for Famine Relief met for the first time. It included representatives of Oxford University, Christian ministers and people with business experience. The committee helped to persuade the government to lift the ban on food going to Greece.

A new organization

The Oxford group was one of many British committees set up to help prevent famine during the war. When the war ended in 1945, most of these groups stopped operating. Europe was once more at peace and life was improving for many people. But the group in Oxford did just the opposite. They began to expand their activities, recruiting more people to help them.

For millions of Europeans, life did not improve quickly once the war ended. Children had lost their parents; families had lost their homes;

farmers looked out on ash where once they had raised crops. Disease was increasing. The Oxford Committee expanded its aims to include 'the relief of suffering in consequence of the war'. In 1948 it began sending supplies and money to relief projects across Europe.

The following year the Oxford Committee realized that Europeans were not the only people who suffered because of wars and disasters. So from 1949, the committee widened its range further, to provide 'the relief of suffering arising as a result of wars or of other causes in any part of the world'.

The organization that we know as Oxfam was born at this time. The committee realized that its full name – the Oxford Committee for Famine Relief – was a mouthful. In those days, organizations had to shorten their names when using the telegraph in the same way that people shorten words when they send text messages today. Their telegraph abbreviation was Oxfam, and gradually people began to use this shortened name instead of the full one. Oxfam became the official title in 1965.

Opposite
As Oxfam looked beyond Europe in the 1950s, it tried to help the many thousands of people made homeless by the Korean War (1950–53) in Asia.

Oxfam shops

Oxfam was the first charity to combine shopping with fund-raising. In 1948 it opened its first shop in Broad Street, Oxford. It was the first full-time charity shop in Britain. Over the years, Oxfam shops have welcomed donations from the public, as well as the time that their volunteers give up to work in them. Oxfam shops provide a valuable source of income for the organization. Just as importantly, they spread the message of what Oxfam is all about. Much of the food and drink sold in Oxfam shops comes from ethical sources and the shops show imagination and flair in their business. Customers can still find bargains in the bookshelves, among the CDs and the wide range of clothing. More recently, Oxfam has opened ten bridal departments, where women can buy wedding dresses for a fraction of the cost of a new one.

Taking centre stage

During the 1950s, Oxfam became a key player in world affairs. It began the decade by committing itself to the biggest project in a developing country outside Europe. Oxfam raised £3500 to help famine relief in the Indian state of Bihar. Then, from 1953 to 1956, it built up a £60,000 fund to help those whose lives were disrupted by the Korean War. In 1959, Oxfam was one of the leading organizations which marked World Refugee Year. The United Nations had called for national organizations to close the European refugee camps which had opened in 1945. Oxfam took direct action, helping many refugees to find permanent homes and publicizing the refugee problem. The Oxford Committee had grown into something bigger and more effective.

An international role

The success of the Oxford Committee, which gradually grew into an international role, inspired people in other countries to follow its example. If Oxfam had branches in other countries it would be far easier to identify problems around the world, and to act quickly.

The Oxford Committee (not yet officially known as Oxfam) began looking for Canadian partners in 1963. Three years later Oxfam Canada was born: it shared the aims and goals of the parent Oxfam, but it was an independent organization.

Other Oxfam branches were formed in the following years. They shared a sense of purpose and a determination to attack poverty throughout the world. Although these national, or regional, branches were determined to remain independent, they formed a confederation – Oxfam International – in 1995.

In just over a decade, Oxfam International has successfully combined relief and campaigning efforts across the globe. In fact, when people refer to Oxfam now, they are almost always referring to Oxfam International and not the original British branch.

In addition to the original Oxfam and Oxfam Canada, Oxfam International has affiliates in the following places: America, Australia, Belgium, France, Germany, Hong Kong, Ireland, the Netherlands, New Zealand, Quebec and Spain.

Unity is strength

The expression 'the whole is greater than the sum of its parts' recognizes how separate elements become more effective when they team up with each other. Ten people who team up may be more than ten times as effective as any one of them would be individually.

The sweeping expanse of the United Nations headquarters looks out across the East River in New York City. Oxfam representatives are experienced at putting their case – and the case of the poor worldwide – at the UN General Assembly.

Former Canadian Prime Minister Lester Pearson helped to lead the Miles for Millions fund-raising march in Canada in 1967. The newly-formed Oxfam Canada helped to organize the event.

Oxfam International works on a similar principle. Together, the 13 affiliates can achieve far more than they could expect to separately. Teamwork and unity are the key words for such a grouping and those ideas spill over into the way Oxfam International deals with the rest of the world. Oxfam also believes that an international approach is needed to deal with international problems: 'With many of the causes of poverty global in nature, the 13 affiliate members of Oxfam International believe they can achieve greater impact through their collective efforts.'

The five rights

Oxfam International believes poor people should not be powerless. They should be able to enjoy the same basic human rights that the rest of us take for granted. Oxfam devotes much of its work to promoting five of these rights:
• the right to a sustainable livelihood;
• the right to basic social services;
• the right to life and security;
• the right to be heard; and
• the right to an identity.

Principles and practice

In September 1996, soon after it was founded, Oxfam International set out its basic aims and approaches in a mission statement. This document contains 18 sections, spelling out the aims and approaches that the different Oxfam affiliates share, and how these beliefs can be promoted through collective action. The mission statement highlights specific areas where Oxfam aims to play an effective role:

• promoting peace;

• helping people push for their own rights;

• making markets more open for poor people to sell their goods; and

• protecting the environment for the benefit of everyone.

Oxfam International has a budget of more than £250 million each year. It operates a small headquarters – its secretariat – from near the organization's original home of Oxford in England. The secretariat also runs offices in four major cities where international decisions are made: Washington, New York, Brussels and Geneva.

Poverty, suffering and injustice are the targets that Oxfam aims to fight on behalf of needy people around the world. People are at the heart of these problems – and solutions – and Oxfam operates with people clearly in mind. Three strands come together to make this strategy successful.

Working with poor people

Poor people are at the heart of Oxfam's work, wherever they live. Oxfam helps people organize to improve their living conditions. It also steps in to help when people face a humanitarian crisis, whether it is natural or man-made.

Influencing powerful people

Oxfam has the power and experience to be heard at the highest levels around the world. It is a voice for the poor. Oxfam can help to change national and international policies so that poor people's lives can be improved.

Joining hands with all people

An international approach means that Oxfam supports the idea of global citizenship – believing that we all have a role to play, and responsibilities to bear, in making the world a better place. Oxfam is skilled at drawing high-profile people into its causes to help publicize its campaigns.

Help where it is needed

Oxfam spends a great deal of money and effort in making long-term plans to improve living conditions for the poorest people in the world. There are many international campaigns which Oxfam has begun or which it supports.

Oxfam makes careful plans at every stage for how it spends money on long-term projects. People's lives can change overnight – or even in a matter of seconds – so responding to emergencies is another very

Muslim Aid, with funding from Oxfam, helps tsunami victims rebuild their houses in the Indonesian province of Aceh. Half a million people in Aceh lost their homes within seconds when the tsunami hit on 26 December 2004.

... ON THE SCENE ... ON THE SCENE ... ON THE SCENE ...

Earthquake efforts

On the morning of 8 October 2005, a huge earthquake ripped through northern Pakistan, killing more than 73,000 people and leaving two million people homeless. The damage to houses, schools, hospitals and roads was hard to calculate, but ran to billions of pounds. A very fast response to the disaster was essential, because the mountainous region expected its first winter snows a few weeks later. Relief organizations raced against time to protect, house and feed the millions of people who were affected.

Oxfam responded quickly to establish a presence in Pakistan which continued for months. It concentrated on a region where 900,000 people badly needed help. Oxfam emergency teams arrived with blankets, tents, clothing, food, water and medicine.

This rapid response saved many lives and helped survivors live through the first winter. Oxfam hygiene kits and specially-built bathhouses helped to prevent the spread of many diseases.

Oxfam's biggest contribution came after the snows began to melt, however. As the Pakistan earthquake began to disappear from world news reports, Oxfam provided farm animals and farming advice so that many families could restart their lives.

The organization also educated young people in the earthquake area. Children were taught about hygiene and protection from disease through games and quizzes. Six-year-old Hummar was a star pupil: 'I learnt to lift the lid of the latrines with my feet because this way I won't get germs on my hands.'

important part of Oxfam's work. The organization makes sure that it is always ready to send staff, money, food or other supplies to disaster areas.

Rapid response

The cost of disasters – both man-made and natural – around the world every year is huge. Oxfam calculates that more than 30 million people are forced to flee their homes every year – that's about the same as the number of people who live in Canada. More than half a million people die in wars and fighting. Some floods and earthquakes can be even deadlier.

The world needs to be able to respond quickly to these emergencies, so that survivors can find some way of returning to their former lives.

Oxfam's international framework allows it to tailor its response to a particular crisis. It can transport staff and volunteers to a disaster zone fast, where they can decide on the best approach. This ensures that disaster victims are given what they need and prevents supply problems such as too many blankets and no tents, for example.

Oxfam works with local governments and with other international relief organizations, as well as with its own affiliates. Over time, these organizations build up skills in particular areas, so they can coordinate their efforts, each undertaking what it does best. Oxfam has built a reputation for providing clean water, or for purifying existing water supplies, in disaster zones around the world.

Children collect supplies from an Oxfam water tank at a Sri Lankan refugee camp. Sri Lanka was one of the countries worst hit by the tsunami of December 2004.

... ON THE SCENE ... ON THE SCENE ... ON THE SCENE ...

Water of life

People can survive for days or even weeks with little or no food. But without water, they may suffer from dehydration in less than a day – especially in hot places. One such place is the Darfur region of Sudan, where millions have been made homeless by a violent conflict that began in 2003. Tens of thousands of people live in refugee camps in the Sudanese desert, and Oxfam teams aim to improve their living conditions. One way they can do this is by delivering fresh water.

Sylvester Ingosi, an engineer working with the Oxfam team in the Gereida camp, was pleased when a system was set up to provide water for the 40,000 refugees who live there. There was a problem, however. The system needed a powerful pump to bring the water up from the ground into a storage tank, and further pumps to send it to different parts of the camp. The pumps ran on diesel, which is expensive and often in short supply.

Ingosi found a way of pumping the water to a storage tank two to three metres above ground on a platform. Then, rather than using diesel, gravity sends the water through pipes across the camp. This system saves more than just diesel. It frees up funds which Ingosi can use elsewhere: 'With the money we could save with this new water supply system, we'd be able to reach more people in even more remote areas – and that way, we can continue to make a real difference to the lives of the people here.'

WHAT DO YOU THINK?

Special advantages
Oxfam has made a name for itself in supplying – or purifying – water supplies in disaster zones. Can you think of any other special advantages it has over other relief organizations?

Seeds of change

Oxfam began as a response to a specific crisis – hunger in wartime Greece – and gradually widened its areas of concern. It continues to deal with specific crises and disasters around the world, but it also continues to widen its focus.

Oxfam workers are now just as likely to be planning strategies for farming communities as supplying blankets to villagers after an earthquake. To understand the thinking behind this approach, imagine how doctors work. Hospitals and clinics are always ready for emergencies – injured or ill people who need urgent treatment. That emergency treatment is like the emergency relief Oxfam provides for people suffering from the effects of a natural disaster or conflict.

But health officials also aim to educate people about hygiene, nutrition, first aid and safety. This sort of knowledge is often called preventative medicine because it helps people to avoid ill health. It also saves governments, hospitals and tax-payers money because it is easier

Oxfam representative Kapitanah Amnah leads a discussion with the men's group in the Philippine village of Lao-Lao. The villagers have suffered from years of conflict in their region.

to plan preventative care than emergency care. Here again, there is a parallel with the work of Oxfam. Helping communities, countries and even regions of the world plan for the future can save lives in the long run and make life more pleasant and healthier in the short term.

What sort of planning?

How can Oxfam prevent problems when people have lived with disaster and hardship for centuries? The answer is through knowledge and teamwork. Oxfam has always valued its contact with local people and organizations. Its development teams do not simply arrive on the scene and tell local people what to do. Instead, Oxfam finds out what it can from local communities, sifting through stories and records to see which problems commonly arise.

Then, because Oxfam has experience around the world, its staff can often suggest solutions that have worked in other areas facing similar problems. A West African solution to drought, for example, could be adapted for people living in the drier areas of India and Pakistan. Or a strategy of crop rotation developed in Indonesia could benefit farmers working in similar tropical conditions in Brazil.

... ON THE SCENE ... ON THE SCENE ... ON THE SCENE ...

Flood response

'Sometimes, even when the sun is out, way up in the hills it's raining and all of a sudden water comes rushing down. It's very dangerous and people can be dragged away in the current; animals are often swept away.'

Luis Mamani Paredes describes the danger that always lies above his home town of Sandia, high up in the Andes Mountains of Peru. Sandia lies inside a steep mountain valley, wedged between a fast-flowing river and a gorge. During the months of the rainy season (November to March) many people in Sandia lie awake at night fearing the worst. Oxfam has worked with PREDES, a local organization, to help people in Sandia prepare for these flash floods – and to learn how to react when they occur suddenly.

One of the most effective parts of this team effort is its youth branch, known as the Jovos (from a Spanish abbreviation for young people involved with disaster prevention). Local teenagers such as Roger Rodriguez Carry and Basty Mesalina Marron Quispe train in first aid and show people escape routes to higher ground and safety.

Oxfam campaigns (see pages 28–31) often support these long-term plans. Spreading the word about how people can improve their lives is an essential part of Oxfam's purpose – its role as a voice for the poor and a link between all the people of the world. Another focus is to help communities keep a sense of dignity. Villagers are prouder of the storage barns they build to store their harvest through dry periods than they would be to receive grain from outside organizations.

Much of this long-term planning lowers the likelihood of disaster. No one can prevent an earthquake, but people can use building techniques which protect houses when earthquakes occur. Farming communities need to find ways to cut firewood without exposing the soil and putting themselves at risk of flash floods. Oxfam often plays a part in this type of disaster prevention.

Opposite
Oxfam helps women, such as this group on the Philippine island of Mindanao, learn more about their basic human rights.

WHAT DO YOU THINK?

How best to help

Like many other international organizations, Oxfam tries to find a balance in how it works with people in developing countries. Some believe that people need to be helped directly with food and money. Others disagree, saying that people will come to depend on handouts and that money should be used to help develop independence. What's your view?

Beginning at home

An old saying goes: charity begins at home. Although this seems a straightforward statement, it can be understood in different ways. For example, some argue that people shouldn't concern themselves with what goes on in other countries and should concentrate instead on improving matters nearer home. This view puts the love of your country in competition with caring for others abroad.

Massive American farms, producing food as if they were factories, receive money from the US government. This makes life harder for farmers in other countries as well as small American farms.

Another view of the saying sees help near home as a first step towards helping the wider world. Oxfam takes this view. It was for many years a British organization, concentrating on problems in Britain's nearest continent of Europe. So, in a sense, Oxfam's charity – which now spans the globe – really did begin at home, or very near home.

Good publicity?

In recent years, organizers of international relief agencies (such as Oxfam) have noticed what they call compassion fatigue in some richer countries – which usually provide most of the agencies' income.

... ON THE SCENE ... ON THE SCENE ... ON THE SCENE ...

Overdue change

Campaigning for change (see pages 28–31) is one of Oxfam's most important roles. With both national branches and international influence, it can listen to people's needs, while pushing to have their voices heard in the wider world. Oxfam America is a leading affiliate raising money and pushing for change. Some of the changes could benefit farmers in the US as much as those in developing countries.

Audrey Arner and her husband Richard live and work on a 100-hectare cattle farm in Minnesota. Like farmers in the developing world, they want to provide food for themselves and earn income from their livestock and crops. But Audrey and Richard grow the wrong crops. Since the 1930s, the United States government has offered billions of dollars to a small number of farmers to grow cotton and grains. Most American farmers, including Audrey and Richard, receive nothing because they do not grow these crops. And the billions of dollars paid to farmers who do grow cotton and grains lead to huge surpluses of cotton and grain sold around the world – making it hard for farmers in poorer countries to sell these crops.

Oxfam America is calling for a change in US farm policy to make things fairer. This would certainly help farmers in developing countries. But it would also release money to help American farmers supply a wider range of farm products in America itself. These small farmers would also find it easier to use traditional farming practices, which protect the environment. As Arner says: 'If we have any compassion at all, we understand what drives people to farm… put yourself behind another farmer's plough to realize the inequality.'

This fatigue seems to result in people cutting themselves off from the rest of the world, as though they have become a bit bored with the subject, having seen so many images of starving children or earthquakes.

One of the best ways to change this view is to show Oxfam working closer to people's own homes. Oxfam International works throughout the world, and not just in the poorest countries (see pages 12–15). Programmes and campaigns in some of the richest countries (see On the scene right) have raised people's awareness of Oxfam. These campaigns should help people in more developed countries, as well as their counterparts in poorer parts of the world.

African cotton producers, who usually work on small farms, suffer when large American and European companies force down cotton prices.

WHAT DO YOU THINK?

Home or abroad
Should Oxfam branches concentrate more on helping their fellow countrymen, rather than focusing on conditions in other countries?

... ON THE SCENE ... ON THE SCENE ... ON THE SCENE ...

Closing the gap

Oxfam Australia has existed only since 2005, but its roots go back much further. The organization began in Melbourne in 1953 as a church-based group called Food for Peace Campaign, which sent donations to a project in India. In 1962 it became known as Community Aid Abroad, and in 1995 it linked up with the Oxfam movement worldwide.

Over more than 50 years, the organization now known as Oxfam Australia has brought attention to the suffering of people in other countries. It combines this with attention to problems in Australia itself. A major campaign in 2007 was called Close the Gap. This refers to the stark difference in health between indigenous people and other Australians.

Indigenous Australians, sometimes called aboriginals, die on average 17 years earlier than other Australians.

Oxfam Australia calls on all Australians to press the government to improve health conditions for these indigenous people. An online petition, which people can sign and send on to elected officials, spells out just how bad the problem is – and also how little money (from the national budget) is needed to improve things. Close the Gap is supported by many famous Australians, including sports stars Cathy Freeman and Ian Thorpe.

The indigenous people of Australia have some of the lowest living standards in their country.

The campaign trail

Oxfam needs to keep a high profile across the world. Its projects need constant funding. The organization also takes its role as the voice of the poor very seriously. People need to know about Oxfam's aims and plans if the organization is to continue to flourish.

The best way to put its message across is to use publicity wisely and skilfully. Oxfam has set up many campaigns to make the world a fairer place. Some of these, such as Make Trade Fair (see page 30), have been supported by international figures. Other campaigns have been equally successful through using a behind-the-scenes approach. Successes in this area include Oxfam's efforts to control weapons and to promote health and education.

Oxfam has the international experience and reputation to press for changes at the highest levels, including among the leaders of the world's richest countries. They are gathered here at the 2006 G8 summit in Saint Petersburg, Russia.

Choosing targets

Oxfam International chose the location of its four campaigning offices carefully (see pages 12–15). The offices are in Washington, New York, Geneva and Brussels. Each of these cities is the headquarters of an international policy-making organization. Oxfam International gains a real advantage from having trained representatives who are experienced at voicing the concerns of the world's poor, based in each city. Below are the key organizations.

Washington: the World Bank and the International Monetary Fund (IMF)

The World Bank, as its name suggests, is a bank that operates around the world. It specializes in offering loans to countries which will help them develop their industries and to improve people's living conditions.

The IMF aims to ensure that the world economy operates as fairly as possible, giving every country an equal chance to buy and sell goods and services.

New York: the United Nations (UN)

The UN is the largest and most respected international organization, with branches and departments which are involved with health, trade, peacekeeping, food, education and many other areas. Its general assembly acts as a sort of world parliament, giving every country the chance to have a say.

Geneva: the World Trade Organization (WTO)

The WTO supervises world trade, trying to make it as free and fair as possible. It organizes international trade agreements, which then become law when passed by parliaments in WTO member countries.

Making trade fair

One campaign that captures the Oxfam message and approach is called Make Trade Fair. Oxfam International uses this slogan to promote international trading justice for the world – not just the richest and most powerful countries (which have often forced other countries to agree to unfair practices).

Make Trade Fair uses Oxfam websites and other promotional methods to provide examples of the unfairness of the existing system and to convince people that it needs to change. The campaign has the support of famous people from all over the world and from all walks of life: this gives the campaign an extra spark of interest and ensures that the media reports on it.

The Make Trade Fair campaign does not merely aim to publicize the issue. It offers clear, workable examples of ways in which the world would operate more fairly if certain actions were taken. These include:
• Richer countries removing barriers to goods coming from poorer countries;

• Ending farm subsidies in richer countries;
• Changing the policies of the World Bank and IMF, so their loans do not come with 'strings attached', or unfair conditions;
• Making patent laws fairer so that poorer countries can afford new equipment and seeds;
• Finding ways to pay fairer prices to small farmers everywhere.

Rice is dumped on Coldplay's Chris Martin, just as cheap rice (grown with US government handouts) is 'dumped' in poor countries driving some rice farmers out of business.

WHAT DO YOU THINK?

Trading fairly

Some people argue that the Make Trade Fair campaign does more harm than good for the poorest countries. By concentrating on selling their goods to richer countries, these critics argue, developing countries simply end up competing with each other. What do you think?

Brussels: the European Commission

This commission is one of the governing bodies of the European Union (EU), made up of 27 European countries. The commission proposes laws for the EU to pass and it acts as a watchdog to make sure EU members keep their promises. The EU is a major trading group and it also has a number of international aid programmes: these two facts are important to Oxfam campaigners in Brussels.

More than one angle

In Africa, the long-running crisis in the Sudanese region of Darfur has spilled over to neighbouring Chad. Across that desert-like region, millions of people have been driven from their homes with only what they can carry – and sometimes with nothing at all. The crisis is acute now, but it will also affect the future, as so much farmland has been trampled or burned.

Oxfam has been involved in the region on many levels and its campaigns reflect this variety of work. Its website pages tell success stories, such as improved water supplies in refugee camps (see page 19). Promoting such work is an important part of Oxfam's job as it helps people realize that Oxfam teams are there to help in the long term. But the scale of the crisis continues to be alarming. That is why in April 2007, newspapers around the world ran large advertisements for Oxfam's Darfur and Chad Emergency Appeal. Stark pictures of homeless families, taken by world-famous photographers, gave an urgency to this vital emergency Oxfam campaign.

Team spirit

Oxfam does not believe that it has all the answers to the world's problems. It has goals and aims – and methods of achieving them – but it also knows when other organizations should take the lead. Oxfam is constantly setting up new partnerships with local groups, and it has a long history of working with other international organizations.

In mid-2007, Oxfam International reckoned that it worked in partnership with about 3250 other organizations around the world. Sometimes the lines are blurred between individual actions by a single organization and a wider team effort with other organizations. Make Trade Fair (see page 30) is a good example. Oxfam's campaign has raised money, enlisted high-profile support and kept the issue of trading justice in the news. But Make Trade Fair is also part of a larger grouping: the Global Call to Action Against Poverty.

Oxfam was one of more than 500 groups that joined forces in 2005 as part of the Make Poverty History campaign. The aim was to publicize the extent of absolute poverty around the world and to pressure governments to do something about it.

This loose alliance of nearly 2000 organizations uses a range of approaches to put across an anti-poverty message worldwide. Make Trade Fair remains an Oxfam International campaign, but its success strengthens the wider alliance. Likewise, people who only knew of the wider aims through another alliance organization could learn about Oxfam's campaign through that route.

... ON THE SCENE ... ON THE SCENE ... ON THE SCENE ...

9 Is Mine

Children in India have established an imaginative campaign to pump more government money into health and education. The 9-is-Mine campaign, operated by children all over India, has collected more than 200,000 young people's signatures. Their aim is to make the Indian government live up to its promise of pledging 9 per cent of its gross domestic product to basic health care and education.

Hollywood star Scarlett Johansson is a lifelong supporter of Oxfam. She travelled to India ito observe Oxfam projects and campaigns. Her reaction after seeing these projects gave a real boost to the 9-is-Mine campaigners: 'Having visited Oxfam-funded school programmes in rural communities has made me realize how vital education is to developing countries in bringing people out of poverty and giving them a sense of dignity, self-worth and confidence.'

Partners, not rivals

Oxfam is just one of many international relief organizations which send teams to disasters and emergencies. These teams share similar goals and do their best to streamline their efforts at disaster sites. Oxfam works with other organizations to produce the most efficient, wide-ranging response to every crisis. In order to do this, Oxfam has arrangements with other organizations which ensure that disaster areas receive the best-quality care.

One of the most important joint agreements is between Oxfam and the International Federation of Red Cross and Red Crescent Societies (IFRC). These two organizations signed a Memorandum of Understanding (MoU) in 1995. It encourages them to share information and training in order to provide safe water, sanitation and good hygiene around the world. The aim is to help affected regions move smoothly from emergency to long-term improvement.

Oxfam and the IFRC were also at the heart of a wider project launched in 1997. The Sphere Project welcomes humanitarian agencies

Lebanon emergency funds

Oxfam has always been proud of the way it accounts for how it spends its money. This good housekeeping is particularly useful when it teams up with other organizations, large and small. After the military violence in southern Lebanon in August 2006, Oxfam joined forces with the Humanitarian Aid Department of the European Commission (ECHO). Their quick response brought essential relief aid to 66,000 people whose lives had been turned upside down by the violence.

Together, Oxfam and ECHO provided the following aid and equipment:

• 3375 hygiene kits
• 1400 toilet cleaning kits (water supplies had been interrupted and disease could spread)
• 1400 solid waste management kits
• 9840 Oxfam-style buckets (containing soap, detergent, candles, matches, cloths and other emergency supplies)
• 900 street waste barrels
• 2296 1000-litre rooftop water barrels

These supplies met specific targets of preventing the spread of disease and maintaining basic fresh water supplies until normal connections could be reestablished.

to join it on a voluntary basis. Together, they can help Sphere map out ways in which agencies can work together in future emergencies. During its first decade, Sphere produced guidelines on the minimum standards which should be met during an emergency. It also acts as a focal point for an exchange of ideas and knowledge about humanitarian relief. Thousands of people representing around 400 organizations from more than 80 countries around the world have helped Sphere develop.

One of many?

Does the world really need so many international organizations like Oxfam? Would the neediest people in the world receive more help if these organizations were combined?

Looking ahead

The threats and dangers facing the world change constantly. For example, during the 1980s few people had heard of the term global warming or of the environmental threat posed by widespread air and car travel. They might rather have been concerned about overpopulation and world hunger. These concerns are still very worrying, but they form part of a pattern of global issues.

Some concerns are tied in with each other. Longstanding problems can become worse as a result of new developments. For example, if global warming continues, then parts of north Africa – and southern Europe – will become too hot and dry for farming. Millions of people will be in danger of going hungry. Rising water levels elsewhere will threaten not just farming, but the very existence of many low-lying coastal regions and islands across the globe.

Protesting at the G8

In July 2005, more than 225,000 concerned people marched on Edinburgh, where the G8 (leaders of the world's eight richest countries) were meeting. They demanded concrete action to tackle world poverty. At the same time, more than three billion people watched the Live 8 concert, which echoed the anti-poverty message.

Oxfam captured the mood by beginning the I'm In campaign to encourage more people to support Oxfam and the wider anti-poverty movement. The public could contact Oxfam by phone, e-mail, text, post or online – and sign the I'm In pledge, which stated: 'I think poverty is an injustice and I want to do something about it.'

Future responses

International organizations, just like families, need to be able to cope with changing circumstances. Oxfam and other relief organizations know that the problems facing the world will not remain the same, so their responses and strategy should also change. In 1997 and 1998, Oxfam stepped back and examined itself so that it could 'develop a strategy so that, no matter how the world changes, it can respond

A lone sunflower blooms in a dry, dusty field. If current global warming trends continue, some of today's richest farmlands will look just as unproductive.

Poverty is a continuing concern in the twenty-first century. These scraps of plastic are this family's only protection against the rain in a favela (slum) in the Brazilian city of Manaus.

and make a major impact on poverty and suffering.' The review prepared Oxfam for the twenty-first century. Oxfam's core beliefs remain the same, although it has streamlined the way the organization is run. With fewer people at the top, Oxfam is better equipped to hear the views of the thousands of people who have a stake in the organization. Oxfam's involvement with other relief organizations and groups of organizations (see page 32) also increased at that time.

So too did Oxfam's involvement with new technology and wider activities. Individual Oxfam affiliates developed websites along with the sites linked to Oxfam International.

Dealing with criticism

Oxfam and other relief agencies are sometimes criticized for the way in which they spend the billions of pounds they raise. Some say that much of the money is wasted, or that it goes into the pockets of agency leaders. In June 2006, Oxfam and ten other NGOs signed the first global accountability charter for the non-profit sector.

Accountability means being able to account for every pound that is received and spent. Signing the charter was just the first step. The organizations also agreed to set up ways to make it easier for the public to check on how well the organizations live up to their promises.

Oxfam has also been the target of criticism. Its Make Trade Fair campaign, for example, led to criticism from two sides. Some other anti-poverty agencies, such as Food First, believe that fighting poverty through more world trade is not the best way to help the poorer countries. They argue that poor countries simply end up competing with each other. The World Trade Organization criticized Oxfam for what they believe was a one-sided account of the WTO position. WTO representatives say that Oxfam has deliberately ignored the valuable technical assistance that WTO gives farmers in the developing world.

This cyber approach informed people around the world about the latest Oxfam campaigns and aims: daily updates and a monthly e-newsletter strengthened this side of Oxfam's operations. Online prompts also offer people an alternative way of donating money to Oxfam.

Taking critcism too far?
An Oxfam report in April 2007 criticized Britain's military presence in Iraq, dating back to the 2003 invasion. It argued that Britain's image around the world would continue to suffer – along with the reputation of organizations such as Oxfam – unless there was a change in policy. Do you think Oxfam was right to criticize the government?

Playing your part

As an organization, Oxfam is all about partnerships, both at home and abroad. Young people are welcome to take part in many Oxfam activities, especially fund-raising efforts.

The 13 Oxfam international affiliates are the best place to learn about how join the wider Oxfam movement. They offer advice on how to make the most of your involvement, and how best to use your skills to make a difference.

An open guitar case is the ideal way to advertise the Oxjam Buskathon, a musical fund-raiser for Oxfam held in Edinburgh in October 2006.

Fund-raising ideas

People are always coming up with interesting, funny and creative ways to raise funds for Oxfam. The Oxfam website offers advice for anyone interested in helping in this way. These are two recent success stories.

Oxjam

This UK-wide series of musical events, including busking, concerts, discos and music downloads received support from thousands of young people, plus bands such as the Futureheads and Scissor Sisters. The first Oxjam in 2006 raised more than £500,000 and it is likely to be repeated in October every year.

Trailwalker

This challenge encourages teams of walkers to complete a tough 100-km walk in less than 30 hours to raise awareness about poverty and suffering. Those who want to take part need to raise sponsorship, which can enable teams to raise more than £1000 each.

Joining forces with an organization such as Oxfam is a great way to harness people's energy and a will to bring about real change. Oxfam International has a special welcome for young people. It offers 300 youth partnerships every year. The 300 young people who become partners every year come from all over the world. Oxfam gives them training and advice on how to put their special skills to the best use locally – and in the world at large.

High-profile role models

Many young people are encouraged to join in once they have seen the example of some of their most admired role models. Hollywood star Danny Kaye began a tradition of linking famous people with good causes when he became a UNICEF goodwill ambassador in 1954. Seeing the face of someone we recognize or admire on a poster or in a newspaper advertisement makes us want to look a bit more closely. If that person is lending support to a good cause, we often consider that cause a bit more closely as well.

Oxfam and Glastonbury

Oxfam is one of three relief organizations to benefit from the Glastonbury Festival (the others are Greenpeace and WaterAid). Michael Eavis, owner of Worthy Farm (the festival site), has welcomed Oxfam since 1993. Oxfam provides the festival with 1400 stewards, who help at entrance gates and in camping areas, directing traffic and monitoring crowds near the stages for safety. The Oxfam stewards are given free entry to the festival, working three eight-hour shifts in return.

The Make Trade Fair shop, donation points and banners keep the Oxfam message prominent across the festival site. Michael Eavis's daughter Rebecca believes this arrangement works well for both the festival and Oxfam.

'Oxfam stewards are always friendly and committed to their cause, without being aggressive about it. Their easy-going attitude is in line with the mood of the festival, and I'm sure it helps generate even more interest in Make Trade Fair and other Oxfam campaigns. Dad also likes to make sure that Oxfam gets a cut of the takings: when the Darfur crisis began, Dad saw to it that Oxfam got a £100,000 donation.' People aged 18 and over who are interested in becoming Oxfam stewards can find out how to apply from Oxfam GB.

Michael Eavis underlines the Glastonbury link with Oxfam. Stewards from Oxfam have worked at the festival since 1993.

Oxfam has been lucky that many famous people – film stars, athletes, political leaders and musicians – offered to help them. The I'm In campaign (see page 37) gained a real boost when former South African president Nelson Mandela supported it in February 2005. Oxfam America called on stars such as Colin Firth, Michael Stipe, Chris Martin and Bono to help raise money for victims of Hurricane Katrina. In April 2006, actress Keira Knightley donated the gown she wore to the Academy Awards ceremony to Oxfam. The gown was auctioned and the money went to Oxfam's East Africa food crisis appeal.

Nelson Mandela teamed up with Oxfam in February 2005.

... ON THE SCENE ... ON THE SCENE ... ON THE SCENE ...

Writing wrongs

Eighteen-year-old Kat Senior, from Swansea in South Wales, has taken time out from her A-level studies to write articles for the Oxfam Generation Why website. The subjects of these articles include young people's involvement with charities, International Women's Day and emergency aid after the 2004 Asian tsunami. Kat says: 'I've always wanted to write, particularly about things that are important to me. I would love to go abroad for my gap year to do voluntary work in Africa or elsewhere and hopefully go on to do journalism or languages at university.'

WHAT DO YOU THINK?

Any ideas?

Can you think of any interesting or unusual ways of raising funds for, or becoming involved with, Oxfam?

Glossary

affiliate A single group linked to a wider organization.

Allies The UK, USA and other countries which fought against Germany, Japan and Italy during the Second World War.

blockade Preventing ships from entering or leaving a country's waters.

charter A written document that outlines the aims of a group.

compassion Care and understanding of other people's needs.

crop rotation A way of planting different crops in fields every year to maintain the soil's fertility.

developing country A country that has little industry and usually relies on basic farming; most developing countries are poor.

environment The natural world around us: the soil, water, air and plants.

ethical Showing concern for justice and fairness.

famine A long period of food shortage, leading to widespread hunger in a region.

General Assembly The branch of the United Nations that acts as a world parliament or congress, with every UN member-country represented.

global warming The rising temperature of the Earth, caused in part by the gases that people pump into the atmosphere.

G8 Short for Group of Eight, a regular gathering of leaders representing the eight richest countries in the world.

humanitarian Concerned with helping other people.

indigenous A native of a country or place.

Korean War A war fought between two Asian countries, North and South Korea, from 1950 to 1953, which also involved UN forces and China.

loan A sum of money that is borrowed, and which must be paid back, as well as extra money, known as interest.

NGO An abbreviation of Non-governmental Organization – an international group or organization that is not governed by any country.

non-profit sector A category of organization that does not aim to make money from its work.

oppression Unfairly harsh action.

overpopulation Too many people to live safely in a region – or in the world.

patent laws Laws that prevent rival companies from using ideas in business or industry.

purifying Cleaning and making safe.

refugee A person who has been made homeless because of war or a natural disaster.

Second World War A war fought from 1939 to 1945 between Germany, Japan, Italy and other countries against the Allies.

steward Someone who helps to keep control and looks after safety at a public event.

summit An international meeting or wider gathering of world leaders.

surplus More than is needed of something.

tsunami A huge, fast-moving wave caused by an underwater earthquake.

UNICEF The United Nations Children's Fund.

Further reading

Let's Eat! Children and Their Food Around the World B Hollyer with Oxfam (Frances Lincoln, 2003)

Looking Behind the Logo: The Global Supply Chain in the Sportswear Industry Oxfam (Oxfam Educational, 2004)

Mapping Our World. Oxfam with R Sudworth (ed) (Oxfam Educational, 2000)

Fed Up: Showing the World You Can Make a Difference 30 Hour Famine with T McLaughlin (Transit, 2004)

Websites

http://www.oxfam.org.uk/coolplanet/kidsweb/index.htm
Oxfam's Cool Planet website with special sections for children and teachers.

http://www.oxfam.org.uk/generationwhy/
Oxfam's Generationwhy site aimed at young people aged 14 and up.

http://www.iyp.oxfam.org/
The site devoted to the Oxfam International Youth Partnerships.

http://www.whiteband.org/
The home page of the wide-ranging Global Call to Action Against Poverty.

Index